INTRODUCTION PARAGRAPH

Hook:	What online video game has over 30 million active users?
Background Information:	According to Wikipedia, Roblox is a mixture of the words "robots" and "blocks."
Personal Experience:	I almost cried when my mom told me to turn off the video game last night.
Build Picture:	My virtual character on Roblox wears a rainbow-colored mohawk and black bandana.
Thesis Statement:	My favorite video game is Roblox because there are fun games to play, interesting people, and cool things to buy.

BODY PARAGRAPH ONE

Topic Sentence:	First of all, my favorite video game is Roblox because there are fun games to play.
SD1: F R E D S:	In fact, most of the games are created by the Roblox community and Roblox employees.
SD2: F R E D S:	Use Roblox Studio in order to create your own game.
SD3: F R E D S:	For example, you can construct bricks made of different colors and shapes.
Concluding Statement:	All in all, my favorite video game is Roblox because there are fun games to play.

BODY PARAGRAPH TWO

Topic Sentence:	Secondly, my favorite video game is Roblox because there are interesting people.
SD1: F R E D S:	Roblox virtual characters are as square as SpongeBob SquarePants.
SD2: CD :	They are like transformers. You can make them change into whatever you want.
SD3: F R E D S:	In fact, you can talk to other players from all over the world on your headset.
Concluding Statement:	Certainly, my favorite video game is Roblox because there are interesting people.

BODY PARAGRAPH THREE

Topic Sentence:	Finally, my favorite video game is Roblox because there are cool things to buy.
SD1: Ⓟ I T :	My Robux account started to shout with glee when my mom deposited 100 robux.
SD2: Ⓢ I D S :	Since I have robux in my account daily, I can buy cool clothes, shoes, and accessories.
SD3: S I Ⓓ S :	"I wish my mom would buy some robux for me too," stated my friend Tommy.
Concluding Statement:	Therefore, my favorite video game is Roblox because there are cool things to buy.

CONCLUSION

Repeat Thesis:	In conclusion, my favorite video game is Roblox because the games are fun, the people are interesting, and there are cool things to buy.
Lesson Learned:	I learned that a virtual world can be fun and interesting just like the real world.
Give Advice:	If you ever play Roblox, make sure you find friends who never bully you.
Final Thought:	Don't get too emotional while playing because it's only a game, not real life.

ELABORATION ACRONYM
FRED'S CD fell in the PIT at SID'S HOME

F	act
R	eason
E	xample
D	etail
S	imile

C	omparison
D	escription

P	ersonification
I	rony
T	extual Evidence

S	ubordinate Phrase
I	nteresting Words
D	ialogue
S	ensory Adjectives

H	yperbole
O	nomatopoeia
M	etaphor
E	xaggeration

INTRODUCTION PARAGRAPH

Hook:

Background Information:

Personal Experience:

Build Picture:

Thesis Statement:

BODY PARAGRAPH ONE

Topic Sentence:

SD1:
_________:

SD2:
_________:

SD3:
_________:

Concluding
Statement:

BODY PARAGRAPH TWO

Topic Sentence:

SD1: _________ :

SD2: _________ :

SD3: _________ :

Concluding Statement:

BODY PARAGRAPH THREE

Topic Sentence:

SD1:

______:

SD2:

______:

SD3:

______:

Concluding Statement:

CONCLUSION

Repeat Thesis:

Lesson Learned:

Give Advice:

Final Thought:

ELABORATION ACRONYM

FRED'S CD fell in the PIT at SID'S HOME

F
R
E
D
S

C
D

P
I
T

S
I
D
S

H
O
M
E

INTRODUCTION PARAGRAPH

Hook:

Background Information:

Personal Experience:

Build Picture:

Thesis Statement:

BODY PARAGRAPH ONE

Topic Sentence:	
SD1: ______:	
SD2: ______:	
SD3: ______:	
Concluding Statement:	

BODY PARAGRAPH TWO

Topic Sentence:

SD1:

_________ :

SD2:

_________ :

SD3:

_________ :

Concluding Statement:

BODY PARAGRAPH THREE

Topic Sentence:

SD1:
______:

SD2:
______:

SD3:
______:

Concluding
Statement:

CONCLUSION

Repeat Thesis:	
Lesson Learned:	
Give Advice:	
Final Thought:	

ELABORATION ACRONYM
FRED'S CD fell in the PIT at SID'S HOME

F
R
E
D
S

C
D

P
I
T

S
I
D
S

H
O
M
E

INTRODUCTION PARAGRAPH

Hook:

Background Information:

Personal Experience:

Build Picture:

Thesis Statement:

BODY PARAGRAPH ONE

Topic Sentence:

SD1:

_________:

SD2:

_________:

SD3:

_________:

Concluding
Statement:

BODY PARAGRAPH TWO

Topic Sentence:

SD1:
______:

SD2:
______:

SD3:
______:

Concluding
Statement:

BODY PARAGRAPH THREE

Topic Sentence:

SD1:
______:

SD2:
______:

SD3:
______:

Concluding
Statement:

CONCLUSION

Repeat Thesis:

Lesson Learned:

Give Advice:

Final Thought:

ELABORATION ACRONYM
FRED'S CD fell in the PIT at SID'S HOME

F
R
E
D
S

C
D

P
I
T

S
I
D
S

H
O
M
E

INTRODUCTION PARAGRAPH

Hook:	

Background Information:	

Personal Experience:	

Build Picture:	

Thesis Statement:	

BODY PARAGRAPH ONE

Topic Sentence:

SD1:
______:

SD2:
______:

SD3:
______:

Concluding
Statement:

BODY PARAGRAPH TWO

Topic Sentence:

SD1:
________:

SD2:
________:

SD3:
________:

Concluding
Statement:

BODY PARAGRAPH THREE

Topic Sentence:

SD1: _________:

SD2: _________:

SD3: _________:

Concluding Statement:

CONCLUSION

Repeat Thesis:

Lesson
Learned:

Give Advice:

Final
Thought:

ELABORATION ACRONYM
FRED'S CD fell in the PIT at SID'S HOME

F
R
E
D
S

C
D

P
I
T

S
I
D
S

H
O
M
E

INTRODUCTION PARAGRAPH

Hook:	
Background Information:	
Personal Experience:	
Build Picture:	
Thesis Statement:	

BODY PARAGRAPH ONE

Topic Sentence:

SD1: __________:

SD2: __________:

SD3: __________:

Concluding Statement:

BODY PARAGRAPH TWO

Topic Sentence:

SD1:
______:

SD2:
______:

SD3:
______:

Concluding
Statement:

BODY PARAGRAPH THREE

Topic Sentence:

SD1: _________:

SD2: _________:

SD3: _________:

Concluding Statement:

CONCLUSION

| Repeat Thesis: | |

| Lesson Learned: | |

| Give Advice: | |

| Final Thought: | |

ELABORATION ACRONYM
FRED'S CD fell in the PIT at SID'S HOME

F
R
E
D
S

C
D

P
I
T

S
I
D
S

H
O
M
E

INTRODUCTION PARAGRAPH

Hook:

Background Information:

Personal Experience:

Build Picture:

Thesis Statement:

BODY PARAGRAPH ONE

Topic Sentence:

SD1:

________:

SD2:

________:

SD3:

________:

Concluding
Statement:

BODY PARAGRAPH TWO

Topic Sentence:

SD1:
______:

SD2:
______:

SD3:
______:

Concluding
Statement:

BODY PARAGRAPH THREE

Topic Sentence:

SD1:
_________:

SD2:
_________:

SD3:
_________:

Concluding Statement:

CONCLUSION

Repeat Thesis:	

Lesson Learned:	

Give Advice:	

Final Thought:	

ELABORATION ACRONYM
FRED'S CD fell in the PIT at SID'S HOME

F
R
E
D
S

C
D

P
I
T

S
I
D
S

H
O
M
E

INTRODUCTION PARAGRAPH

Hook:

Background Information:

Personal Experience:

Build Picture:

Thesis Statement:

BODY PARAGRAPH ONE

Topic Sentence:

SD1:
_________:

SD2:
_________:

SD3:
_________:

Concluding Statement:

BODY PARAGRAPH TWO

Topic Sentence:

SD1: _______:

SD2: _______:

SD3: _______:

Concluding Statement:

BODY PARAGRAPH THREE

Topic Sentence:

SD1: __________ :

SD2: __________ :

SD3: __________ :

Concluding Statement:

CONCLUSION

Repeat Thesis:	

Lesson Learned:	

Give Advice:	

Final Thought:	

ELABORATION ACRONYM
FRED'S CD fell in the PIT at SID'S HOME

F
R
E
D
S

C
D

P
I
T

S
I
D
S

H
O
M
E

INTRODUCTION PARAGRAPH

Hook:

Background Information:

Personal Experience:

Build Picture:

Thesis Statement:

BODY PARAGRAPH ONE

Topic Sentence:

SD1: _________:

SD2: _________:

SD3: _________:

Concluding Statement:

BODY PARAGRAPH TWO

Topic Sentence:

SD1:

_________:

SD2:

_________:

SD3:

_________:

Concluding
Statement:

BODY PARAGRAPH THREE

Topic Sentence:

SD1:
_________:

SD2:
_________:

SD3:
_________:

Concluding Statement:

CONCLUSION

Repeat Thesis:	

Lesson Learned:	

Give Advice:	

Final Thought:	

ELABORATION ACRONYM
FRED'S CD fell in the PIT at SID'S HOME

F
R
E
D
S

C
D

P
I
T

S
I
D
S

H
O
M
E

INTRODUCTION PARAGRAPH

Hook:

Background Information:

Personal Experience:

Build Picture:

Thesis Statement:

BODY PARAGRAPH ONE

Topic Sentence:

SD1: __________:

SD2: __________:

SD3: __________:

Concluding Statement:

BODY PARAGRAPH TWO

Topic Sentence:

SD1: ______:

SD2: ______:

SD3: ______:

Concluding Statement:

BODY PARAGRAPH THREE

Topic Sentence:

SD1:
______:

SD2:
______:

SD3:
______:

Concluding
Statement:

CONCLUSION

Repeat Thesis:	

Lesson Learned:	

Give Advice:	

Final Thought:	

ELABORATION ACRONYM
FRED'S CD fell in the PIT at SID'S HOME

F
R
E
D
S

C
D

P
I
T

S
I
D
S

H
O
M
E

INTRODUCTION PARAGRAPH

Hook:	

Background Information:	

Personal Experience:	

Build Picture:	

Thesis Statement:	

BODY PARAGRAPH ONE

Topic Sentence:	

SD1: ________:	

SD2: ________:	

SD3: ________:	

Concluding Statement:	

BODY PARAGRAPH TWO

Topic Sentence:

SD1: _______:

SD2: _______:

SD3: _______:

Concluding Statement:

BODY PARAGRAPH THREE

Topic Sentence:

SD1:
_________:

SD2:
_________:

SD3:
_________:

Concluding
Statement:

CONCLUSION

Repeat Thesis:

Lesson Learned:

Give Advice:

Final Thought:

ELABORATION ACRONYM
FRED'S CD fell in the PIT at SID'S HOME

F
R
E
D
S

C
D

P
I
T

S
I
D
S

H
O
M
E